IMAGES OF
CARDIFF, NEWPORT AND
THE VALLEYS RAILWAYS

IMAGES OF
CARDIFF, NEWPORT AND THE VALLEYS RAILWAYS

CLASSIC PHOTOGRAPHS FROM
THE MAURICE DART RAILWAY COLLECTION

HALSGROVE

First published in Great Britain in 2012

British Library Cataloguing-in-Publication Data
A CIP record for this title is available from the British Library

ISBN 978 0 85704 157 9

HALSGROVE
Halsgrove House,
Ryelands Business Park,
Bagley Road, Wellington, Somerset TA21 9PZ
Tel: 01823 653777   Fax: 01823 216796
email: sales@halsgrove.com

Part of the Halsgrove group of companies
Information on all Halsgrove titles is available at: www.halsgrove.com

Printed in China by Everbest Printing Co Ltd

CONTENTS

ACKNOWLEDGEMENTS

I express special thanks to my friend Kenneth Brown for permission to reproduce photos taken by him. Likewise I express thanks for permission to use photos which I have purchased from the collections of the Stephenson Locomotive Society, The Locomotive Club of Great Britain (Ken Nunn collection) and Rail Archive Stephenson (Photomatic). Also my thanks and apologies are proffered to other photographers whose work has been used and not credited. Where no credit is given the photographer is unknown. I also extend my thanks to Steve Jenkins for advice when describing some of the carriage and wagon stock. I am also indebted to Simon Butler of Halsgrove for suggesting the idea of this series of books.

REFERENCE SOURCES

A Detailed History of British Railways Standard Steam Locomotives. RCTS.

British Railways Locomotive Stock Changes and Withdrawal Dates. 1948 –1968.
    Michael McManus.

British Railways Tunnels. Alan Blower.

Great Western Railway Locomotive Allocations for 1921. Ian Harrison.

Great Western Railway Locomotive Allocations for 1934. Nigel Pocock and Ian Harrison.

GWR, LMSR and BR Locomotive Allocations for various years. RCTS.

GWR Locomotive Allocations. First and Last Sheds. 1922 – 1967. J. W. P. Rowledge.

Industrial Locomotives of Gwent. Geoffrey Hill & Gordon Green.

Industrial Locomotives of Mid & South Glamorgan. Geoffrey Hill.

Locomotives of the Great Western Railway. Various parts. RCTS.

Official Handbook of Railway Stations etc. Railway Clearing House.

British Railways Bridges & Viaducts. Martin Smith.

The Directory of Railway Stations. R. V. J. Butt.

Track Layout Diagrams of the Great Western Railway and BR Western Region.
    R. A. Cooke.

The Railways Of Great Britain. A Historical Atlas. Colonel M. H. Cobb.

My personal notebooks dating from 1945.

INTRODUCTION

At a very early age I was taken to Dockyard Halt, near Devonport and soon afterwards to St Budeaux GWR station to 'watch trains'. I was taught to remember the names of three engines that passed through. At home there was a Hornby Gauge '0' model railway. Most Saturday afternoons my parents would take me with them from St Budeaux to either Devonport, reached by tram, or Plymouth, to which we caught a 'Motor Train' to Millbay. So my interest in railways steadily developed. During the summers of 1937, 1938 and 1939, the three of us spent a week travelling by train to Torquay, Paignton or Goodrington, with sometimes a venture to Kingswear and across to Dartmouth on the 'MEW' or to Dawlish Warren. We used a Family Holiday Runabout ticket for the week and set out from St Budeaux on an excursion train that ran daily from Saltash to Paignton and which, from memory, was usually hauled by a Castle class locomotive to Newton Abbot.

From our front windows at Higher St Budeaux I was able to watch trains in the distance as they climbed towards the Devon side of the Royal Albert Bridge. They could also be seen as they rounded the curves west of Saltash station. I asked my father on one occasion why we did not go to Cornwall instead of to Paignton and he replied that it was better to go up the line. This was probably because there was a daily excursion train from Saltash to Paignton although we sometimes had to change trains at Newton Abbot and cross over the footbridge. My father would bring home books about railways. They had been loaned to him for me to look at and they contained many photographs of railway subjects. During the Second World War, following the second batch of blitz raids on Plymouth when many schools were damaged, I was evacuated to Bude by train from Friary. I stood in the corridor for most of the way to 'see where I was going' much to the consternation of the WVS ladies who were accompanying us. I recall seeing a tank engine, at what I later learned was Meldon Quarry, carrying 500S on its tank side. This was the T class 'Service loco'. Whilst at Bude I began to hear about places such as Holsworthy and Okehampton, which I had passed through on the train. Evacuation to Bude was followed by a short period back at St Budeaux after which I spent two years at St Austell, using trains to and From North Road. Whilst there, at the evacuated Grammar school, I met many older boys who were railway enthusiasts and my 'railway education' commenced properly.

In August 1946 my mother and I took a day trip to Cardiff as I had heard and read so much about the Severn Tunnel. We found our way to Canton shed and I went up on the footbridge where several local boys were gathered. I asked them if they had been around the shed and they told me that you were ejected if caught. However, after a while when most of them had left I chanced it and went down the steps and in between lines of locos as we did at Laira. I went around the long shed and was halfway around the Roundhouse when I met the Foreman. He challenged me and I replied in my Devon accent and he laughed and told me to carry on. On the way to Cardiff, from Newport onwards there was almost a continuous string of Goods trains buffer to buffer as Permissive Working was in operation. So that was my introduction to South Wales. I was most impressed.

My father had been transferred from Devonport to the Dockyard at Gibraltar during 1943, and in the summer of 1947 I went there by sea for a holiday for several weeks. My father was an amateur photographer and he taught me to use a box camera. I immediately started taking photographs of Gibraltar Dockyard locomotives from a balcony! On returning to St Budeaux I found my father's two old cameras and managed to obtain a film for each. A large folding Kodak that used A-122 film turned out to have a pin hole in the bellows, only discovered when the results of the first film were seen. This made it unusable. The other was an old Box Brownie which had a push-over lever shutter release and had one good and one faulty viewfinder that showed two images, one above the other. I persevered with this but did not know enough to achieve much success. I tried to record trains passing through St Budeaux and went to Laira shed late in September and took photos, some against the low evening sun. Still, we all had to learn by experience. With those which I had taken at Gibraltar, this was the start of my collection of railway photographs. I saved my pocket money and managed to go on a few Saturday trips to Exeter and as a holiday treat I was allowed to make trips to Bristol and Salisbury. In January 1948 my mother and I joined my father in Gibraltar which involved sailing from and to Liverpool.

In June 1951 I ventured west of Cardiff to reach Llanelly and discovered a different part of the Welsh railway network. Then in 1954 I spent a few days exploring lines west of Llanelly and reached Fishguard and Neyland. Later, my employment took me to lodge at St Austell where I finally took up permanent residence. As time progressed I was able to buy better cameras and commenced longer railway trips to places further afield. My railway interest widened from purely collecting engine names and numbers to encompass signalling and railway history. This was progressed by meeting more very knowledgeable older railway enthusiasts and railwaymen, many of whom became lifelong friends. After several day trips to South Wales sheds in the mid-1950s I spent a fortnight in Wales in September 1957. I worked my way up and down and across the Valleys to Neath from where I headed to Brecon. from there I headed to Oswestry and across to Machynlleth, later progressing to Barmouth for a few nights. From there I headed south to Carmarthen via Aberystwyth, which I had already visited a few days previously. I had been bitten by the Welsh bug and felt that I was beginning to know my way around the area reasonably well. The area covered in this book is unique for the density of traffic operating over many lines which converged at the three centres of Newport, Cardiff and Barry. The four track section through the Taff Vale was a prime example of the facilities provided to handle the enormous volume of coal trains passing Down loaded and returning Up empty. In this area descending south through a valley were always referred to as Down with heading north being 'Up' although operationally the converse applied. At Easter 1962 I spent a week in Ireland travelling out via Fishguard and returning via Holyhead. I have returned periodically including visits with friends who drove their car which enabled exploration of places well off the beaten track. I developed a desire to obtain photographs of some of the locomotives that I had seen in my early years, so the process of searching for and purchasing photos commenced. As my interest and knowledge grew, so likewise did the quest for more photos. This now encompassed all of Devon and Cornwall and large sections of Wales, along with various classes of locomotives from all over the country. An interest in Narrow Gauge and Industrial railways developed. So the 'Archive' steadily grew from filling an expanding suitcase to occupying a considerable expanse of shelf space in two rooms. When it was suggested that I compile some books making use of some of these images I thought that it would be a great idea as many of them, to the best of my knowledge, had not previously been used in publications. Previous books covered Devon, Cornwall, Somerset and Dorset, Wiltshire and Hampshire and Lancashire & Cheshire. With so many photos available the choice has been difficult but constraints such as copyright and previous use have been considered.

This is not an attempt to include every location or type of locomotive that has worked in the area but is simply a selection from my collection. As the photos have been collected by me personally my own particular interests and likings for certain locomotive types are reflected by some sections containing larger numbers of photos than others. Some older historic images are included but I have attempted to give a good overall coverage of the area from the 1880s to the present day. I have included large selections of locos which were absorbed by the GWR along with GWR tank locos at the expense of main line express types which worked through the area. Tank locos will forever be associated with 'The Valleys'. A few BR diesels and industrial locomotives are included. So many photographs of the preservation era have been published that I have avoided this period. I have also used some items which are not photographically perfect but merit inclusion because of their content. These images may be of great interest to modellers of historic locomotives with period layouts. As this book features images from my personal collection, the layout follows the order in which the collection is arranged. This follows locomotive wheel arrangement and types from the largest downwards in decreasing order of size, with a few exceptions. It is a system that was used in the past by several notable authors that presents a markedly different layout to the now standard practice of following routes geographically. Readers seeking photos at specific locations should refer to the index of locations at the end of the book. I have used the Anglicised versions of places which were in general use during the period covered in this book. I have attempted to make the captions detailed without delving too deeply into railway history or becoming too technical. Any errors that are discovered are purely attributable to myself. I trust that within the contents there is material to cater for most railway interests and that memories of a bygone age will be recalled.

Maurice Dart
St Austell 2012

1

2–8–2 TANKS AND 2–8–0s

The heavy tank locos worked Main line and some Valley line Goods trains. 2-8-0s worked Main line Goods traffic.

We commence with the large impressive GWR 7200 class 2-8-2Ts and 7213 from Aberdare shed waits at Pontypridd to work back home on 26 June 1960. This loco has a raised Frame over the cylinders. The Driver is waiting patiently for his Fireman to return from the station Buffet with some tea as they await a path onward to Abercynon. Maurice Dart/Transport Treasury

Above: In the mid-1950s Ebbw Junction's 7218 waits for the road at Newport High Street with a Goods which is probably empty Hopper wagons for Ebbw Vale.
Maurice Dart

Left: At home at Radyr shed on 17 April 1960 is 7242. To its rear, also at home is 5101 class 2-6-2T 4160.

Below: Three locos are at home at Radyr shed on 17 April 1960. In the foreground is 7252 with 5101 class 2-6-2T 4143 to its rear. The Large Prairie is mainly concealed by 6400 class 0-6-0PT 6434.
Maurice Dart/Transport Treasury

We progress to GWR 2-8-0s. On 30 June 1957 at Ebbw Junction shed is ex-Works 2800 class 2-8-0 2831 from Aberdare with locally based 8750 class 0-6-0PT 3712 to its rear. Mike Daly

On 30 June 1957 2800 class 2861 is at home on Ebbw Junction shed. To its left is 4-6-0 5939 'TANGLEY HALL' from Old Oak Common. Maurice Dart

On 28 August 1960 2884 class 2-8-0 3865 from Oxley shed (Wolverhampton) waits in Severn Tunnel Junction Up Middle yard to back onto a heavy Goods. Maurice Dart

This section ends with a shot of grimy WD 2-8-0 90218 waiting for the road at the west end of Newport High Street on 30 June 1957. As this loco was allocated to Woodford Halse shed this photo confirms the adage that one can never predict exactly what one will see anywhere on the railway. Waiting at the platform to depart with a Down express is 4-6-0 5094 'TRETOWER CASTLE' from Gloucester shed. Maurice Dart/Transport Treasury

2

2–8–0 TANKS

These worked Intermediate Goods trains over the Main line routes and also in the Western and Eastern Valleys.

Three 4200 class locos at home at Newport Pill shed on 30 June 1957 are 4233, 4211 and 4291. Maurice Dart/Transport Treasury

At home on shed at Severn Tunnel Junction on 31 March 1957 is 4200 class 4217. Brian Webb Collection/Industrial Railway Society

4200 class 4233 and 4211 are at home at Newport Pill shed on 30 June 1957. The first loco has been rebuilt with a raised Frame and outside Steampipes. Maurice Dart/Transport Treasury

A loaded Coal train, probably from Marine colliery, headed by 4200 class 4237 drifts down through Aberbeeg station on 1 September 1957. The loco was allocated to Aberbeeg shed which was some distance south of the station. Maurice Dart

Two locos at home on shed at Aberbeeg on 1 September 1957 are 5205 class 5241 and 4200 class 4277. Having walked to the shed from Aberbeeg station when I had finished 'going around' I walked south alongside the track to Llanhilleth station to board a train to return to Newport. Maurice Dart

Neath shed's 4200 class 4282 on an Up mixed Goods approaches Newport High Street on 2 September 1957. A fine set of signals are on the gantry on the right. Maurice Dart

The crew relax in the cab of 5205 class 5224 between shunting at Severn Tunnel Junction West Up yard on 5 June 1960. The loco was allocated to Severn Tunnel Junction. Maurice Dart/Transport Treasury

In the early 1950s 5205 class 5262 brings an Up mixed Goods though Severn Tunnel Junction where the loco was based.

3

0–8–2 TANKS AND 0–8–0s

These worked heavy Goods traffic over their pre-grouping company's lines. The LNWR 0-8-0s also worked excursion trains at weekends.

Barry Railway H class 0-8-2T GWR 1382 is at home at Barry shed in the mid-1920s. Withdrawal was in September 1928.

A crowded Barry shed contained BR H class 0-8-2T GWR 1383 which was at home in the mid-1920s, probably on a Sunday. The loco was withdrawn in August 1930. H. C. Casserley

At home at Barry shed in the early 1920s is BR H class 0-8-2T 83 which became GWR 1384. This loco was withdrawn during July 1930. Locomotive Publishing Co. Ltd.

In the early 1920s at Barry shed BR H class 0-8-2T 84 which became GWR 1385 is at home. Withdrawal came in June 1928.

On 17 November 1923 BR D class 0-8-0 GWR 1387 is shunting at its home shed, Barry. This loco was withdrawn during November 1927.

The same loco GWR, ex BR D class 0-8-0 1387 is seen from the other side at home at Barry shed in the mid-1920s. Also present is locally based BR B1 class 0-6-2T 269 which survived until October 1949 and 5205 class 2-8-0T 5225 from Ebbw junction shed.

In the late 1920s BR D class 0-8-0 GWR 1390 is at home at Barry shed. This loco worked until April 1930. Real Photographs

Left: Approaching Barry on 9 June 1957 LNWR G2 class 0-8-0 49409 from Tredegar shed heads the empty stock for a return excursion from Barry Island to the Sirhowy Valley. The train has just passed Barry Works. Its route home would probably have been via Wenvoe, Tynycaeu Junction, Penrhos Junction, Aber Junction, Hengoed and Pontllanfraith. Mike Daly

Below: On 5 January 1958 a special train for the Stephenson Locomotive Society is about to enter the east portal of 302 yd long Clydach tunnel on its way to Merthyr. The train is headed by a LNWR 0-8-0 which is piloted by a LNWR Coal 0-6-2T. The line closed completely the following day. R. Stewartson/Stephenson Locomotive Society

4–6–0s

These mainly worked passenger trains over the Main lines.

On 30 June 1957 Castle class 7037 'SWINDON' from Swindon shed restarts a Down express from Newport High Street.
Maurice Dart/Transport Treasury

On 4 September 1956 a visitor inside the Roundhouse at Pontypool Road shed is Newton Abbot's 6814 'ENBORNE GRANGE'. To its right is local 8750 class 0-6-0PT 3717.
Transport Treasury

Two locos are in Godfrey Road sidings opposite Newport High Street station on 28 August 1960. Centre is 6818 'HARDWICK GRANGE' from Llanelly shed with, to its left Llantrisant's 8750 class 0-6-0PT 9746. Maurice Dart/Transport Treasury

Wolverhampton Stafford Road shed's 6856 'STOWE GRANGE' waits to depart from Cardiff General with a Down express in the late 1930s.

In the mid-1930s Star class 4021 'BRITISH MONARCH' from Shrewsbury shed waits to depart from Cardiff General on a Down working. Until 1927 this loco was named 'KING EDWARD' after which it carried 'THE' in front of 'BRITISH' for a few months. A GWR Horsebox is next to the loco. A. G. Ellis

Around 1922 Star class 4029 'KING STEPHEN' from Old Oak Common shed awaits departure from Cardiff General with an Up express. In 1927 this loco was re-named successively 'THE SPANISH MONARCH' followed by 'SPANISH MONARCH'. This loco was withdrawn in November 1934. Locomotive Club Of Great Britain/Ken Nunn Collection

Heading an Up Parcels train in the 1920s at Severn Tunnel Junction is Saint class 2916 'SAINT BENEDICT' from Bath Road shed, Bristol. Withdrawal took place in July 1948. The loco is coupled to GWR Low Siphons and a GWR Bogie Siphon.

Around 1953/54 1026 'COUNTY OF SALOP' from Bath Road shed takes an Up local Passenger train out of Newport High Street.

A surprise loco at Pontypool Road shed on 18 August 1962 was Royal Scot class 46129 'THE SCOTTISH HORSE' which was allocated to Crewe North shed. The loco had originally been named 'COMET'. At this period of time some trains from Liverpool and Manchester were worked by ex-LMS locos as far as here. Maurice Dart/Transport Treasury

GWR SMALL PRAIRIE TANKS

The 4500 and 4575 class locos worked Passenger trains on the Eastern and Western Valley lines and also on the Cardiff Valley lines from the early 1950s when 'Interval Auto services' were introduced. A few of the 3901 class found there way to the area where they were used on Passenger and Goods turns.

We commence with 4500 class 'Small Tank' 45s. On 23 July 1962 4507 from Yeovil Town shed waits at Caerphilly Works to receive attention.

In 1950 4514 is at home at Aberbeeg shed. The loco does not carry a GWR ABEEG shed stencil and has not been fitted with a 86H shedplate. Kenneth Brown

Two locos at home at Ebbw Junction shed in September 1936 are 4500 class 4518 which retains Inside Steampipes and 4800 class 0-4-2T 4821. The Loco Repair Shops are in the left background. Note the unusually placed toolbox on the front end of the Running Plate. Norman Preedy Archive

Around 1946 Ebbw Junction shed's Non-Auto fitted 4524 waits on two Auto coaches at the west end of Newport High Street. This loco was transferred to Laira shortly afterwards where, on arrival it caused us great excitement as it carried NPT shed stencils which were soon replaced by LA stencils. B. K. B. Green/Initial Photgraphics

At home at Pontypool Road shed on 19 July 1953 is 4533. R. K. Blencowe Collection

We now progress to 'Large Tank' 4575 class locos and Auto-fitted 4580 is at home at Cathays shed on 21 April 1957. 0-6-0PTs in the background are, from the left, 6400 class 6434 (Merthyr), 7400 class 7445, 8750 class 4698 and 6400 class 6435 which were Cathays locos. Maurice Dart/Transport Treasury

Locos at home on shed at Cathays on 21 April 1957 are Auto-fitted 4589 and 7400 class 0-6-0PT 7445. The Loco Repair Shop is in the background. Maurice Dart/Transport Treasury

Local engine 4593 is shunting in the Carriage sidings at Pontypool Road on 30 March 1959.

Maurice Dart/Transport Treasury

On 1 September 1957 5544 is at home outside the shed at Aberbeeg. Maurice Dart/Transport Treasury

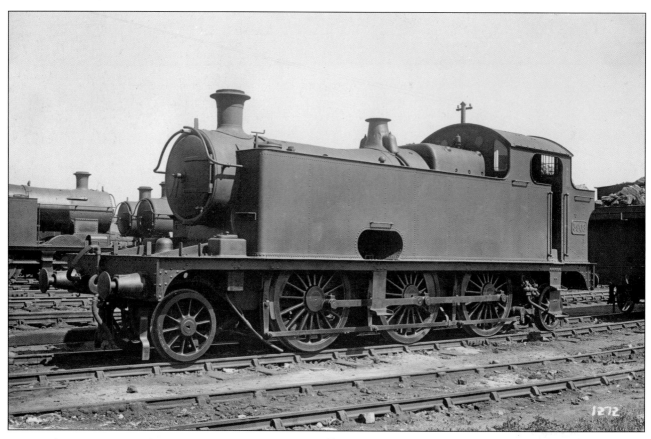

Late in the 1920s 3901 class 3908 is at home at Barry shed. This loco which was rebuilt from Dean Goods 0-6-0 2497 was withdrawn in September 1930. F. Moore's Railway Photos

6

GWR ABSORBED PRAIRIE TANKS

These worked Goods traffic over lines owned by their originating company which was the Alexandra Docks (Newport) Railway. In their latter years they were used as Shed Pilots.

On 23 May 1954 1205 is at home at Cardiff Canton shed where it was used as Shed Pilot. L. R. Peters

In the 1930s 1206 is at home at Newport Pill shed.

Ex Mersey Railway bought by the ADR, GWR 1207 rests with a similar loco at Newport Pill shed on 10 October 1926. This loco was withdrawn in May 1932.

Another ex Mersey Railway loco bought by the ADR, 1211 is at home at Newport Pill in the mid-1920s. This loco was withdrawn in September 1929. Real Photographs.

7

GWR LARGE PRAIRIE TANKS, AN LMS 2–6–2 TANK AND 4300 CLASS 2–6–0s

The Large Prairies worked Passenger trains up the Rhondda Valley and also to Rhymney and Barry. They were also used on Parcels trains on the Main line and on Piloting duties through the Severn Tunnel. The LMS tank worked on the Sirhowy Valley line. GWR Moguls worked Parcels and Goods traffic on the main lines.

Left: This section commences with 3150 class 2-6-2Ts. Standing forlornly awaiting cutting up at Caerphilly Works on wet and misty 3 September 1957 3163 had been withdrawn from Gloucester shed several weeks earlier on 10 June. Maurice Dart/Transport Treasury

Below: On 30 June 1957 3170 is at home on the coal stage line at Ebbw Junction shed. Maurice Dart

An Up Mixed Goods pulls out of Severn Tunnel Junction West Up yard on 8 April 1950. The train engine, 5600 class 0-6-2T 6676 is piloted by 3172. both of the locos were allocated to Severn Tunnel Junction. B. W. L. Brooksbank/Initial Photographics

Four locos are at home at Severn Tunnel Junction shed on 9 September 1956. From the left they are 5101 class 2-6-2T 5155, 3177, 3150 and 2800 class 2-8-0 2844. Owing to their constant use piloting trains through the Severn Tunnel the shed's 3150 class tanks were only ever clean when they returned from a visit to a Works. R. J. Buckley/Initial Photographics

Above: In the late 1950s locally based 5101 class 2-6-2T 4119 pilots a 4300 class 2-6-0 on an Up coal train as it passes through Severn Tunnel Junction station. J. Davenport/Lakeside (Windermere) Railway Society

Left: Awaiting cutting up in an area behind and below Barry Works on 26 June 1960 is 5101 class 2-6-2T 4164 which had been withdrawn from Severn Tunnel Junction on 27 February. I was delighted to locate this loco which had managed to elude me. Maurice Dart/Transport Treasury

One of the five members of the 3100 class, Ebbw Junction's 3103 moves 'Light engine' through Newport High Street on 2 September 1957. Maurice Dart

Two LMS locos are at home at Pontypool Road on 30 June 1957. Centre is Stanier 3MT 2-6-2T 40091 which had been transferred in from Abergavenny when that shed closed. Peeping out from the shed is Swindon built 8F 2-8-0 48415. Maurice Dart

Gloucester shed's 4300 class 2-6-0 6309 takes a Down Parcels train through Newport High Street on 31 August 1952. Maurice Dart

A big surprise at Radyr shed on 17 April 1960 was 4300 class 2-6-0 6377 which was a Carmarthen engine. The Foreman said that it was on its way to Caerphilly Works. However it is not contained in the list of locos dealt with at Caerphilly! To its left, at home is 9400 class 0-6-0PT 3409. Maurice Dart/Transport Treasury

8

5600 CLASS 0–6–2 TANKS

These locos were the GWR 'Workhorses of the Valleys' where they worked both Passenger and Goods trains. Normally between 75% and 80% of the class of 200 locos operated from South Wales sheds. They were built to a similar design to that used by many of the absorbed companies whose earlier locos they replaced. So this large section pays tribute to them. Two varieties of steam heating pipes which were fitted to the many of the locos could be located on either side beneath the running plate.

Two locos at home alongside the coal stage at Cathays shed on 21 April 1957 are 5600 class 5601 and 5101 class 2-6-2T 4177 both of which sport copper capped chimneys. On the coal stage the left of the pair is an ex LNER Sleeper wagon. Maurice Dart/Transport Treasury

Below: On 18 April 1954 5602 is at home at Canton shed, Cardiff. A. C. Gilbert

One very wet 27 August 1960 5605 which was allocated to 88D (Merthyr) is shunting wagons on the siding to the opencast coal site at Cwmbargoed. The code 88D also applied to sheds at Rhymney, Dowlais Central and Dowlais Caeharris. This loco was working from Caeharris. Maurice Dart/Transport Treasury

Above left: Rain was pelting down and bouncing off objects when I took this shot of two locos at home at Caeharris shed on 27 August 1960. Nearest is 5610 whilst 5618 is sheltering inside the shed. In this dire weather a driver offered to move 5610 outside the shed for me. I thanked him and took this shot as I liked the aspect. Also I was becoming somewhat waterlogged! Maurice Dart

Above right: On 26 June 1960 5612 from Llanelly in on shed at Barry having worked in on an excursion to Barry Island. The string of locos on the left, which are all at home are, from the nearest, 5637, 8750 class 0-6-0PT 8764, 5700 class 0-6-0PT 7764, 6619, 6697 which is preserved and 9400 class 0-6-0PT 9425. Maurice Dart/Transport Treasury

Four of the class at home at Radyr shed on 17 April 1960 are 6626, 5618, 6608 and 6660.

Maurice Dart/Transport Treasury

A railway journal early in 1960 contained a photograph taken from an excursion train from Rhymney to Barry as it crossed Walnut Tree viaduct. The train ran on Summer Sundays only in 1959 and covered much non-passenger mileage, avoiding Caerphilly and Cardiff. As I would be returning from two weeks holiday near the end of August in 1960 I wrote to the Stationmaster at Rhymney and enquired if the train was running on Sunday 28 August. The reply came back in the affirmative also stating that this would be its last date to operate in 1960. I was using a Circular Tour ticket for my travels and included the route in my specification. The ticket arrived with a note attached which stated 'No fare is available for the section of route designated' and I was 'to purchase a ticket at Rhymney to cover that section of the trip'. Having

visited Rhymney shed in the morning and had drinks in the Railway Club with the train's Fireman I was locked into a compartment to give me complete freedom to take photos from either side of the train. Passengers trying to come aboard were most puzzled at my compartment being locked! Also it was a non-corridor coach and having consumed the contents of three bottles of cider I was very pleased to reach Barry! Here is the 12 Noon Summer Sundays only excursion from Rhymney to Barry Island entering 490yd Walnut Tree (Garth or Garth Woods) tunnel hauled by Rhymney's 5622 on 28 August 1960. The route was via Aber Junction, Penrhos Junction, Walnut Tree viaduct and Tynycaeu Junction to Cadoxton. This was the last occasion on which the train ran over this route. The line through the tunnel closed in 1963 with that on the viaduct following in 1967.

Maurice Dart/Transport Treasury

On 3 September 1957 5632 is at home at Treherbert shed alongside the coal stage. Maurice Dart

At Rhymney shed in steam as 'spare' loco for Ballast trains on 28 August 1960 is Barry shed's 5636. On the right is GWR 10 compartment non-corridor 3rd class coach W1848W. Maurice Dart/Transport Treasury

With two sets of driving wheels removed on 21 April 1957 5640 from 88D is laid up in the yard at Cardiff East Dock shed. The loco would probably have been working from Rhymney or Caeharris sheds. Maurice Dart/Transport Treasury

On 17 April 1960 5648 is at home at Radyr shed. Maurice Dart

Three of the class at home inside Caeharris shed on 19 August 1962 are 5652, 5655 and 5666.

Maurice Dart

Two more of the class at home inside Caeharris shed on 19 August 1962 are 5660 and 5671.

Maurice Dart/Transport Treasury

Standing outside its home shed at Caeharris on 2 September 1957 is 5666. The right hand line extended through the shed to access a turntable used to turn locos for work with a snow plough in the winter. At this time the coal stage was on the other side of the running line to the shed and can be partially seen on the left. Maurice Dart

Lurking at home in the back of Caeharris shed on 19 August 1962 is 5671.
Maurice Dart/Transport Treasury

In the mid-1950s 5674 allocated to 88D (probably Caeharris) is outside Caerphilly Works after receiving an overhaul and repaint. Stanley J. Rhodes

Locos at home at Abercynon shed on 26 April 1953 include 5682 and Taff Vale 'A' class 0-6-2T 356.

On 17 April 1960 5683 rests at home on shed at Radyr. This loco had been repainted in 'Green Lined Out' livery. Maurice Dart/Transport Treasury

Aberdare shed's 6605 waits to depart from Aberdare High Level on 18 August 1962 with a service to Pontypool Road. Maurice Dart/Transport Treasury

In the early 1950s 6619 from Barry shed heads a Passenger service near Heath Halt.

A train from Aberdare High Level to Nelson & Llancaiach enters Quakers Yard High Level on 13 August 1957 hauled by 6628 From Aberdare shed. B. K. B. Green/Initial Photographics

Pontypool Road shed's 6634 stands at Crumlin Junction on 18 August 1962. It was waiting to return to Llanhilleth on the Western Valleys line where it was acting as Banker for trains climbing to Crumlin High Level.

Maurice Dart/Transport Treasury

Below: On 14 April 1955 Radyr shed's 6635 blasts up the Roath Branch with a train of empty coal wagons from Cardiff Docks.

S. Rickard/Top Link Photocards

In the 1950s 6637 is at home near the coal stage at Barry shed. Stanley J. Rhodes

Standing on the 'Hump' at Severn Tunnel Junction Up Hump sorting box on 17 April 1960 is 6642 which was allocated to Severn Tunnel Junction shed. Maurice Dart/Transport Treasury

Barry shed's 6643 brings an Up service carrying Target 80 into Cardiff Queen Street on 3 September 1957. The gantry carrying signals for both directions is prominent together with a water tank and a Down starter signal. Maurice Dart

Left: On 31 July 1965 'The Rambling 56' Railtour organised by Swansea Railway Circle was worked by 6643 which by now was officially allocated to Llanelly shed although the loco is devoid of a shedplate. Among routes it visited was the line from Penrhos Junction to Tynycaeau Junction which was truncated at the east end of Walnut Tree tunnel. The train has stopped for photography on Walnut Tree viaduct before returning to Penrhos Junction. Note the Check Rails on the outside of each line and the rust covered line on the left. Maurice Dart

Two locos at home at Barry shed in the late 1930s are 5622 and 6647. Another member of the class is mostly hidden.

Sporting 'Green Lined Out' livery 6648 along with 6608 is at home at Radyr shed on 17 April 1960. Maurice Dart/Transport Treasury

Visiting from Pontypool Road shed 6653 is at Ebbw Junction shed on 6 January 1957. One of the sheds 9F 2-10-0s, possibly 92001, is partly visible in the background. Brian Webb Collection/Industrial Railway Society

Three locos at home at Barry shed around 1947 are 5621, 6668 (with a BRY shed stencil) and 5700 class 0-6-0PT 6745.

On 31 August 1952 6673 from Severn Tunnel Junction shed waits to depart with vans from Godfrey Road yard, Newport. Maurice Dart/Transport Treasury

The ECS for an excursion from Blaenavon Low Level to Barry Island passes northbound though through Panteg & Griffithstown on 24 June 1956 hauled by Pontypool Road shed's 6675. R. J. Buckley

9

GWR ABSORBED 0–6–2 TANKS

These were the 'Workhorses of the Valleys' prior to the introduction by the GWR of the 5600 class locos. However some were not completely displaced by the newcomers and maintained a presence in the area until the mid-1950s. Many were rebuilt at Swindon Works and gained GWR fittings. I have attempted to pay them due justice in this large section. The numbers quoted are those allocated by the GWR unless stated otherwise. I have quoted the dates for locos which were withdrawn before 1950.

Alexandra (Newport & South Wales) Dock Railway 0-6-2ST 190 is at home at Newport Pill shed in the 1930s. Withdrawal occurred in April 1948.

Barry Railway K class 196 built by the Cooke Loco Corp. in the USA is at home at Barry shed around 1930. This loco was withdrawn in May 1932.

Barry Railway B class 226 is at home alongside the coal stage at Radyr shed on 21 June 1937. Withdrawal came a few months later in November.

In 1937 Barry Railway B1 class 245 is at home at Barry shed around 1930. This loco was withdrawn in May 1932. To its left is 4200 class 2-8-0T 4200 which was working from Ebbw Junction shed in the early 1920s.

Barry Railway B1 class 240 from Barry shed is on the coal stage road at Radyr in July 1949. The loco is sporting its GWR CV BRY shed stencil. L. R. Peters

Brecon & Merthyr Railway 0-6-2ST1677 waits to depart from Merthyr on a train to Brecon around 1922. The loco which was probably allocated to Brecon shed was withdrawn during September 1928.

Two Cardiff Railway locos, 152 and 154 are at home alongside the coal stage at Cardiff East Dock around 1930. 152 was withdrawn in December 1936. Following withdrawal in June 1934 154 was sold to R. Frazer & sons. Ltd in September of that year.

Cardiff Railway 155 is at home at Cardiff East Dock around 1949. In addition to an 88B shedplate the loco carries its GWR CV CED shed stencil. In the left background is GWR Cardiff East Dock Breakdown van No.177. Stanley J. Rhodes

In the late 1920s Rhondda & Swansea Bay Railway 167 from Danygraig shed keeps company with Duffryn Yard's 5205 class 2-8-0T 5251 at Treherbert shed. Withdrawal for 167 came in September 1936. Railwaymen paused between duties whilst the photographer operated. He was probably using a tripod, possibly with a plate camera.

Rhondda & Swansea Bay Railway 179 from Duffryn Yard shed is on the turntable at Treherbert in the early 1930s. Withdrawal took place in June 1936.

Around 1952 Rhymney Railway R class 37 is at home with previously seen Cardiff Railway 155 at Cardiff East Dock. Stanley J. Rhodes

Rhymney Railway R class 38 is at home at Cardiff East Dock on 21 April 1957.
Maurice Dart/Transport Treasury

On 12 January 1956 Rhymney Railway R class 42 is at home at Cardiff East Dock.
Brian Webb Collection/Industrial Railway Society

Four locos are at home at Cardiff East Dock shed in mid-1956. Centre is Rhymney Railway R class 43. To its left are 9400 class 0-6-0PTs 8464 and 3406. In the right background is 8750 class 0-6-0PT 6765. P. H. Groom

Only a week or so before withdrawal Rhymney Railway A1 class 53 is at home at Cardiff East Dock on 19 June 1949.

Cardiff East Dock's Rhymney Railway A1 class 54 is at Ferndale shed on 5 July 1936. Withdrawal took place in April 1948. R. J. Buckley/Initial Photographics

Above left: In June 1936 Rhymney Railway A class 57 and 58 are on shed at Radyr. In 1934 57 was working from Cardiff East Dock and 58 was based at Barry.

Above right: With its rear Driving wheels removed Rhymney Railway A class 59 is at home outside the lifting shop at Cardiff East Dock on 24 August 1954. Maurice Dart

Rhymney Railway A1 class 66 looks quite clean at home at Cardiff East Dock where it was working as 'Shed Pilot' on 24 August 1954. On the right is ex Private Owner 21T Mineral wagon P19429. Maurice Dart

On 9 August 1931 Rhymney Railway AP class 81 is at home at Rhymney shed.

During early 1927 Outside Framed Rhymney Railway M class 0-6-2ST 106 is dumped at Cardiff Docks following withdrawal in October 1926.

Outside Framed Rhymney Railway 57 class 0-6-0PT 136 is at Rhymney shed in the early 1930s. This loco was withdrawn from Cathays shed in June 1934. Locomotive & General Railway Photographs

At home at Cardiff Docks in the early 1920s is Outside Framed Rhymney Railway 57 class 0-6-0ST 137 which was withdrawn during December 1927. To its left is Outside Framed 57 class 0-6-2ST 148 which was also withdrawn in December 1927.

Above left: Taff Vale Railway O4 class 289 is at home at Abercynon on 16 October 1934. This loco survived until August 1949.

Above right: Taff Vale O4 class 293 carrying a GWR CV RYR shed stencil is at home at Radyr shed in July 1949.

L. R. Peters

In the mid-1930s Taff Vale A class 299 is at home at Abercynon shed.

Taff Vale A class 304 (402 until 1947/8) is at home at Abercynon shed in July 1957. Terry Nicholls

Taff Vale O4 class 111 which became GWR 314 simmers at Pontypridd around 1920. The loco was probably working from Cardiff East Moors shed. This loco worked until September 1949.

During a visit by the Stephenson Locomotive Society to Treherbert shed in 1935 Taff Vale O4 class 321 (later 218) from Ferndale was present.

About 1920 Taff Vale A class 12 which became GWR 344 awaits departure from Cardiff Queen Street. This engine was based at Penarth Dock shed in 1922.

Taff Vale A class 75 which became GWR 347 waits to depart from Cardiff Queen Street around 1921. This loco was based at Cathays.

Taff vale A class 91 which became GWR 351 waits to depart from Cardiff General in 1920. In 1921 this loco was based at Treherbert.

In July 1957 Taff Vale A class 373 is at home at Abercynon shed. Terry Nicholls

Taff Vale A class 376 is at home at Rhymney shed late in 1954. Stanley J. Rhodes

Taff Vale A class 159 which became GWR 381 waits on a train at Barry Town in 1920. This engine was based at Cathays in 1921. A. C. Roberts

On shed at Canton, Cardiff in July 1949 are Taff Vale A class 381 and Taff Vale O4 class 203 (formerly 310). Both locos were allocated to Canton. L. R. Peters

Taff Vale A class 382 is at home at Barry shed in the early 1950s. A non GWR standard 'Not to be moved' notice is attached to the engine.

Around 1920 Taff Vale A class 162 which became GWR 383 waits to depart from Cardiff Queen Street. This loco was based at Cathays shed.

Four locos are at home at Abercynon shed on 9 June 1957. From the left they are 1600 class 0-6-0PT 1620, Taff Vale A class 383, Taff Vale A class 304 (ex 402) and 8750 class 0-6-0PT 9642. Maurice Dart/Transport Treasury

In the early 1950s Taff Vale A class 389 from Barry shed brings a train into Barry Island where the service will terminate.

On 23 May 1954 three locos at home on shed at Cathays are Taff Vale A class 391, Auto-fitted 4575 class 2-6-2T 4580 and 5600 class 0-6-2T 5670. L. R. Peters

In July 1957 Taff Vale A class 398 is at home at Abercynon shed.

Terry Nicholls

At home at Treherbert shed on 13 June 1932 is Taff Vale O4 class 409 (later 218). The shed Foreman wearing a trilby hat is posing alongside the loco.

Around 1920 Taff Vale A class 410 which became GWR 399 waits on a train at Barry Town. This loco was based at Cathays shed.

Around 1920 Taff Vale A class 415 which became GWR 406 and then 307, has arrived at Treherbert on a train. This was a Cathays loco.

This large section ends with Taff Vale U1 class 30 which became GWR 602 at Barry Town in 1914. In 1922 this loco was working from Cathays shed and was withdrawn during May 1931.

10

LMS 0–6–2 TANKS

These mainly worked passenger and freight trains over the Sirhowy Valley and associated lines.

There were ten LNWR 'Coal Tanks' at home at Abergavenny shed mid-morning on 25 August 1952, eight of which were 'in store' in two rows alongside the shed. A line of wagons unfortunately blocked most of the outside row preventing photography. Included in this shot are 58915, 58924 and 58925. This was my first sighting of these venerable old locos and this was my second shot learning to use my father's metric graduated Zeiss-Ikon camera. Maurice Dart/Transport Treasury

Probably in the 1930s 'Coal Tank' 7765 is in the yard at Abergavenny shed. It appears to be carrying a 6B Mold Junction shedplate.

This remarkable photo from the early 1920s shows an unidentified 'Coal Tank' hauling a 'Pochin Collier's train' composed of 20 elderly short wheel base carriages up the Sirhowy valley line. It is nearing Pochins Pits sidings and miners platform which was an unadvertised station in use from 1922 until 1960.

11

0–6–0s

Various generations of these types worked light passenger and Goods trains throughout the area.

Sporting a tender from an ex ROD 2-8-0 Ebbw Junction's 2251 class 2227 waits with a service from Brecon to Newport at Ponsticill Junction on 11 September 1951.

On 26 April 1948 Ebbw Junction's Dean Goods 2407 brings a short Down Goods through the bleakly situated Dowlais Top.

W. A. Camwell

8750 class 0-6-0PTs and a 5600 class 0-6-2T keep company at Merthyr shed with visiting Dean Goods 0-6-0s 2516 and 2538 which were on 'special train' duty in the early 1950s. Both of the 0-6-0s were allocated to Oswestry. Peter Gray

Whilst travelling north to Liverpool on 7 April 1966 as I approached Pontypool Road I saw three withdrawn locos stored at the site of the closed and demolished loco shed. Some days later I carried out a series of visits to loco depots despite the weather having deteriorated with heavy snow falling. I had decided to de-train at Pontypool Road and saved my last shot of the holiday to record the locos. I attempted to follow the old route to the loco shed and ended up to my knees in snow. I managed to cross the main lines where the foot crossing was

completely buried in snow and approached the locos which were at the south end of the snowbound yard. On 15 April 1966 here are withdrawn 4F 0-6-0 44449, Black 5 4-6-0 45142 and 8F 2-8-0 48273. They had been withdrawn from Workington, Crewe South and Trafford Park sheds. To end the story I was unable to find overnight accommodation at Pontypool but luckily found a bus going to Newport where I found solace in an hotel where the bedrooms were heated by hot water pipes. So I managed to dry my socks, shoes and trousers overnight and have some much needed food!

12

GWR 5700 CLASS 0–6–0 PANNIER TANKS

These useful locos were to be found working a variety of duties throughout the area. The exception was the 67XX series which were purely shunting locos and were fitted with a steam brake and 3 link couplings.

In the late 1950s 5775 and 5756 are at home at the south end of crowded Pontypool Road shed. 5775 is preserved at the Keighley & Worth Valley Railway. Stanley J. Rhodes

Mid-morning on 2 September 1957 5777 from Newport Pill shed loiters alongside Tredegar shed. Maurice Dart

At home at Cardiff East Dock shed on 27 July 1950 is 6700 which is standing alongside the shed's breakdown vans. B. W. L. Brooksbank/Initial Photographics

In the late 1930s 6703 is at home at Cardiff East Dock shed. The top of an elevator can be seen above the rear of the loco.

Shunting in Cardiff Docks amid typical surroundings in the early 1950s is Cardiff East Dock's 6705. This was one of the four members of the 67XX series that I saw whilst on a day trip from St Budeaux to Cardiff in 1946.

In the late 1930s 6707 is at home at Cardiff East Dock keeping company with Rhymney Railway 0-6-2T 44 from Radyr shed.

In the early 1930s 6726 is at home at Newport Pill shed keeping company with resident Brecon & Merthyr Railway 0-6-2T 504 which was withdrawn in January 1948. Beyond the loco on the right is GWR Loco Coal wagon 23080.

One of the early arrivals at Woodham's scrapyard at Barry and was cut up there was 6736 which had been withdrawn from Swindon shed. It is at Woodham's yard on 26 July 1960 with dismantling beginning. This was another of the four locos of the 67XX series which I saw during my 1946 trip to Cardiff. Maurice Dart/Transport Treasury

At home at Newport Pill shed in the mid-1950s are 6739 and 5734. Stanley J. Rhodes

Following withdrawal by BR several members of the class were purchased for further use by the National Coal Board. I attempted to locate some of them but several were inside dark sheds which made photography most awkward. On 31 March 1972 7714 which had been withdrawn from Birkenhead shed at the end of December 1958 is in the shed at Penalltau Colliery in a rather woebegone condition. Nonetheless this loco has been preserved at the Severn Valley Railway. Maurice Dart

Above left: Shunting past Pontypool Road Station South Signal Box in the afternoon on 18 August 1962 is local engine 7724 which I recorded from the loco shed yard. Maurice Dart/Transport Treasury

Above right: Three locos at home at Abercynon shed on 26 June 1960 are 7744, 5600 class 0-6-2T 5686 and 1600 class 0-6-0PT 1612. Maurice Dart/Transport Treasury

Another of the class sold to the NCB was 7754 which had been withdrawn from Wellington shed in December 1958. Devoid of its cabside number 7754 in immaculate green livery stands outside the NCB loco shed at Talywain having completed its duties in the afternoon on 4 April 1969. Wheels from headgear lie in the foreground. The loco carried a front buffer beam number. This loco is preserved on the Llangollen Railway. Maurice Dart

On 26 April 1953 7766 is at home on shed at Merthyr.

In the mid-1930s 8711 from Ebbw Junction shed stands at the west end of Newport High Street station. Godfrey Road Goods station is in the background. Much manual labour will be required to load the large number of small containers on carts into railway vans.

Local engine 8735 is at home over the ash pits alongside the coal stage at Abercynon shed on 26 June 1960. Maurice Dart

GWR 8750 CLASS 0–6–0 PANNIER TANKS

These were a modernised version of the 5700 class locos and performed similar duties. The 67XX series were regarded as purely shunting engines and were fitted with 3 link couplings and a Steam Brake.

In the mid-1950s 3634 from Ebbw Junction shed brings a local Passenger train into the west end of Newport High Street.

Three locos are at home at Pontypool Road shed on 18 August 1962 by the ash pits alongside the coal stage. From the left they are 4603, 3683 and 4-6-0 4958 'PRIORY HALL'.

Below: In January 1963 local engine 3705 has had a snow plough attached at Newport Pill shed. This loco lived at Laira and St Blazey sheds for many years so was a familiar sight to me.

Probably around March 1963 local engine 6756 also has a snow plough attached at Newport Pill shed.

On 5 June 1960 6765 is at home over the ash pits at Barry shed. Maurice Dart/Transport Treasury

Whilst I was visiting Pontypool Road shed during the afternoon of 18 August 1962 locally allocated 8781 was on the opposite side of the main lines shunting at the gas works. The loco is coupled to a GWR Shunter's truck.
Maurice Dart/Transport Treasury

In the late 1950s 9618 from Merthyr shed stands at the west end of Newport High Street station. B. K. B. Green /Initial Photographics

On 2 September 1957 I found my way to Dowlais Central station where I saw the loco shed across the track. As I had a permit to visit the shed I crossed the track and found the small shed empty. After some minutes I found a railwayman and had a chat. He told me to walk out along the track until I came to some sidings where I would find some locos. So mid-afternoon at Guest. Keen & Nettlefold's Sidings, Dowlais are 3767 from Brecon shed, 9665 from Hereford shed and 9643 which was the local resident. I was amazed to find three locos from widely different sheds shunting at this remote location. Maurice Dart/Transport Treasury

The 8.50am Newport to Blaenavon train halts at Pontypool Crane Street on 24 June 1956 hauled by 9667 from Ebbw Junction shed. R. J. Buckley

170. Early in 1962 9678 which is carrying a 88H (Tondu) shedplate stands outside the roundhouse at Aberdare shed. Stanley J. Rhodes

Yet another loco sold to the NCB was 9792 which was withdrawn from Neath shed in April 1964. This loco is inside the ruinous NCB shed at Mardy Colliery in 1973. This loco was sold for scrap during July or August of that year.

14

6400 AND 7400 CLASS 0–6–0 PANNIER TANKS

The 6400s worked Auto services in the valleys. They were fitted with a screw reverser which was a distinct asset when working these trains. The 7400s worked mainly as Pilots at loco depots and yards and also worked local Goods trains.

Outside the large Factory at Ebbw Junction on 19 June 1960 is the shed's 6401 which had been withdrawn from service the previous day.

Transport Treasury

On an inclement day in 1955 6402 from Cathays shed has arrived at the branch terminus at Coryton with an Auto train from Cardiff Queen Street. R. Stewartson/ Stephenson Locomotive Society.

On 23 May 1955 Ebbw Junction's 6409 waits on a Auto train at Severn Tunnel Junction with what is probably a working for Tintern.

Carrying the BRITISH RAILWAYS legend on its tanks Abercynon shed's 6411 has arrived at the pastoral branch terminus at Old Ynysybwl Halt on 11 September 1951 with Auto coach 114. H. C. Casserley

In the afternoon sun on 17 April 1960 6411 rests at home at Radyr shed. Maurice Dart/Transport Treasury

Below: Aberdare shed's 6413 waits with an Auto train in one of the Down Loops at Pontypool Road on 25 August 1952. This was my first shot using my father's metric graduated Zeiss-Ikon camera which I had borrowed for the holiday and had to learn to use. Maurice Dart/Transport Treasury

An old friend of mine, 6417 was a Laira engine for many years. It was transferred to Aberdare shed so I was delighted to find it at Pontypridd waiting to work the Auto train I intended catching to Abercynon on 9 June 1957.

In a photographically awkward position 6423 is at home at Cathays shed on 4 April 1948.

On 3 January 1959 Ebbw Junction's 6426 has arrived at snowy Nantybwch on a train from Newport. Nantybwch No.1 Signal Box is prominent. Stephenson Locomotive Society

Merthyr shed's 6427 waits at Ponsticill Junction to return home with a one coach train on 29 May 1957. The loco is coupled to Auto trailer W249W. R. K. Blencowe Collection

In the late 1930s 6429 rests at home outside the south end of Pontypool Road shed.
W. Leslie Good

Above left: Photographed from a passing train whilst resting at home at Severn Tunnel Junction shed on 5 June 1960 is 6430. This loco was transferred to Laira in 1962 for around seven months and I was hauled by it on Auto services. It has been preserved and works on the Llangollen Railway. Maurice Dart/Transport Treasury

Above right: In the evening on 18 August 1962 6433 rests at home inside Merthyr shed. Steam, smoke and light created an unusual effect above the loco. Maurice Dart

Three locos rest at home on shed at Radyr on 17 April 1960. They comprise 6434, 7200 class 2-8-2T 7252 and 5101 class 2-6-2T 4143. Maurice Dart/Transport Treasury

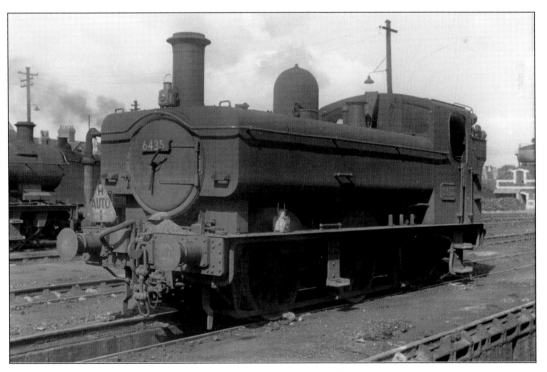

In August 1953 surprisingly without a shedplate and still carrying a barely readable GWR CYS shed stencil at the top of the footstep 6435 is at home at Cathays shed. This loco has been preserved and now forms part of the operational fleet on the Bodmin & Wenford Railway. Transport Treasury

Six locos are visible on shed at Merthyr on 23 June 1960. Identifiable is local resident 6436. Gantry signals protect the approach to the station.

Abercynon shed's 6438 approaches the branch terminus at Coryton with the 10am Auto train from Penarth on 15 November 1957. This loco was transferred to Laira in 1962 for nine months and hauled Auto trains which I used.

Transport Treasury

On 20 December 1963 grubby 7403 rests at home on shed at Severn Tunnel Junction. On the right is GWR Breakdown van DW91. R. K. Blencowe Collection

In the early 1950s Hereford shed's 7420 shunts the small yard at Dolygir. Hugh Davies

I recorded long time Aberdare shed resident 7423 from a passing train on 18 August 1962. It is shunting at Aberdare High Level station yard. Maurice Dart/Transport Treasury

On 9 May 1964 Aberdare shed's 7435 was at home on the coal stage line. R. K. Blencowe Collection

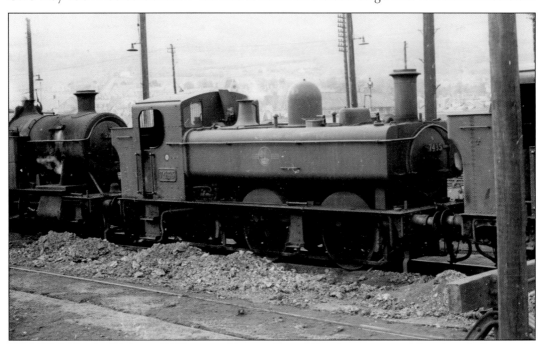

15

9400, 1500 AND 1600 CLASS 0–6–0 PANNIER TANKS

The 9400 class locos worked on similar duties to the 8750 class locos. The 1500 class short wheel base locos mainly worked in Docks where tight radius curves existed. The 1600 class worked on lines with restricted loading gauge which existed in Industrial Estates and at other locations.

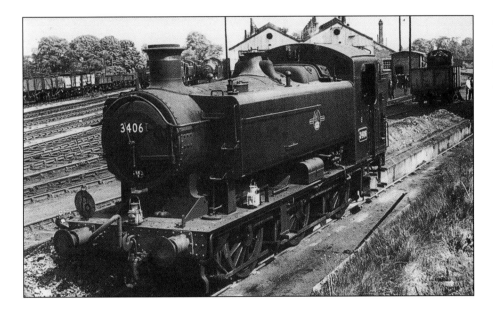

On 31 May 1962 9400 class 3406 is at home on the coal stage road at Radyr shed.

John Goss/J. V. Prints

At home at Radyr shed on 17 April 1960 is 9400 class 3409. To its left are 5600 class 0-6-2Ts 6686 (Radyr) and 5600 (Treherbert or Ferndale).

Maurice Dart/Transport Treasury

On 13 August 1957 a short Goods is being shunted back into sidings at Quakers Yard High Level by Aberdare shed's 9400 class 8444. B. K. B. Green/Initial Photographics

Two locos at home at Radyr shed on 17 April 1960 are 9400 class 8471 and 5101 class 2-6-2T 4143. Maurice Dart/Transport Treasury

Two locally based engines at home on shed at Ferndale on 3 September 1957 are 9400 class 9425 and Auto-fitted 4575 class 2-6-2T 5574. Maurice Dart

Two locos at home at Newport Pill shed on 30 June 1957 are 1500 class 1507 and 5700 class 0-6-0PT 6727. Maurice Dart

This photo presents a mystery. Having spent the night at Caerphilly, as I travelled to Rhymney on the morning of 28 August 1960 I saw a Pannier Tank across the valley outside the NCB loco shed at Elliot Colliery. I photographed it on the return trip and identified it as a 1600 class loco. However no loco of that class is recorded as working at this colliery at that time. 1604 had been on 'on loan' to Elliot early in the year but was returned to Swindon from Abercynon by April. 1600 was purchased by the NCB in 1959 and was at Nine Mile Point

Colliery. Could this have been loaned to Elliot? Another possibility is that either 1653 or 1656, both of which were allocated to Ebbw Junction was 'on loan' to the colliery for a short period. Maurice Dart/Transport Treasury

Left: Four locos are at home on shed at Abercynon on 5 June 1960. They are 1600 class 1641, 5600 class 0-6-2T 5682, 8750 class 0-6-0PT 3783 and 5600 class 0-6-2T 5686. Maurice Dart/Transport Treasury

16

OLDER GWR 0–6–0 PANNIER TANKS

These were the forerunners of the later locos and performed similar duties. Some of these retained 'half cabs' and some received 'full cabs'.

At home on shed at Pontypool Road on 20 March 1938 are 2721 class 2728 and 2021 class 2077. Withdrawal occurred in April 1948 and February 1947. L. Hanson

Llanelly shed's 2721 class 2730 is in the yard at Caerphilly Works in the 1930s. Withdrawal occurred in April 1948. Note the pile of boiler tubes in the foreground.

In the early 1930s Merthyr's 2721 class 2732 shunts in the yard near its home shed. This loco was withdrawn in October 1945. Locomotive & General Railway Photographs

Cardiff Canton allocated 2721 class 0-6-0ST 2740 brings an Up Goods through Cardiff General early in 1920. This loco, which received Pannier tanks in October 1920 was withdrawn from Truro shed in October 1945. Luckily I saw it in 1944 or 1945.

In the 1930s 2721 class 2750 is at home at Merthyr shed. This loco was withdrawn during November 1945.

A. G. Ellis

In the early 20th century excursions were operated at times from Merthyr to Aberystwyth via Brecon, Moat Lane Junction and Machynlleth. Around 1922 one these is climbing near Cefn Coed hauled by Merthyr's 2721 class 2766. This loco worked until November 1945.

The Locomotive Club Of Great Britain/Ken Nunn Collection

On 30 July 1939 2721 class 2794 from Aberbeeg shed is at Ebbw Junction. This loco worked until November 1949.

In August 1954 2181 class 2183 (ex 2074) awaits attention at Barry Works. This loco was at Croes Newydd in the early 1950s but was transferred to Newton Abbot, where I saw it, for a short period.

2021 class 0-6-0ST 2035 is at Newport Pill shed in the early 1930s. It was allocated to Cardiff Canton in 1934 and received Pannier tanks in May 1936.

In the 1930s Pontypool Road shed's 2021 class 2080 has arrived at its home station with an Auto train.

In the early 1920s 2021 class 0-6-0ST 2098 from Merthyr shed waits to depart from its home station on a service to Cardiff. This loco gained Pannier tanks during September 1925.

850 class 1966 was sold to a colliery company following withdrawal in July 1939. In 1950 it was recorded working at Risca Colliery. I was lucky to see this loco in September 1957 inside the NCB loco shed at Tredegar. Kenneth Brown

At home on shed at Barry on 19 June 1949 are 850 class 1993 and 8750 class 0-6-0PT 6754. A. N. H. Glover

At home on shed at Ebbw Junction on 31 May 1936 is 1854 class 1890 which succumbed in June 1947. F. K. Davies

At Canton shed in the late 1930s at home is 1854 class 1891 which worked until December 1949.

In 1930 850 class 871 is at home at Ebbw Junction shed. This loco was withdrawn in July 1931.

On 22 April 1905 645 class 0-6-0ST 770 waits to depart from Newport on an Up Passenger service. Withdrawal took place in October 1936. The Locomotive Club Of Great Britain/Ken Nunn Collection

In the late 1930s 1854 class 1800 rests at home at Ebbw Junction shed where I luckily saw this loco in August 1946 as I passed by in a train. Withdrawal came in December 1947. J. G. Sturt

Outside Framed 1076 'Buffalo' class 965 shunts at Cardiff General in the mid-1920s. This loco was withdrawn in January 1930.

GWR ABSORBED 0–6–0 TANKS AND AN LNER 0–6–0 TANK

The locos which were absorbed by the GWR mainly operated over the their original company's routes although some ended up sold into industry following withdrawal. This same fact also accounts for the presence of a solitary LNER loco in this section.

Alexandra Dock & Railway Co. 0-6-0T 666 is at home at Newport Pill shed in 1948. Part of the transporter bridge can be seen on the right of the photo. Kenneth Brown

This unusual photo is believed to depict the remains of Alexandra Dock & Railway Co. 0-6-0ST 668 in 1948 at Deep Navigation Colliery. This loco was withdrawn in February 1929 and sold to the Ocean Coal Co. at Treharris. It was scrapped at the colliery between 1947 and 1949. Kenneth Brown

Barry Railway A class 0-6-0T 703 was withdrawn in May 1932 and was sold to Lady Windsor Colliery near Ynysybwl three months later. It was recorded working at the colliery in the late 1940s. Scrapping took place in 1956. B. K. B. Green/Initial Photographics

This is another shot from the late 1940s of Barry Railway A class 0-6-0T 703 shunting near Lady Windsor Colliery, Ynysybwl. In the left foreground is Llanbradach Colliery 7 plank Mineral wagon 434.

Barry Railway F class 0-6-0PT 721 was withdrawn in December 1934 and was sold to Treorchy Railways in May 1935. This system served collieries in the Cwmparc valley. The loco was recorded at Treorchy on 14 October 1949. Scrapping took place during 1953/54. B. K. B. Green/Initial Photographics

In the 1920s Barry Railway E class 0-6-0T 782 slowly moves a train on the Breakwater Railway at Barry Island over the movable level crossing over the line from Barry Island to Barry Pier adjacent to the east portal of Barry Pier tunnel. This loco was withdrawn in June 1939 and was sold to the Harton Coal Co. five months later. It worked at Boldon Colliery and was scrapped March 1958. The

main lines though the tunnel closed in 1975. As an adjacent signal box closed in May 1929 this indicates the date when use of the Breakwater line ceased. The line entered a tunnel immediately to the right of the photo.

Barry Railway E class 0-6-0T 783 is at home under repair with its rear driving wheels removed outside the 'Tank shed' at Barry shed on 6 July 1947. The loco was withdrawn during August 1948.

Still lettered GWR Burry Port & Gwendraeth Valley Railway 0-6-0ST 2196 'GWENDREATH' from Llanelly shed is awaiting attention at Caerphilly Works on 6 July 1952. B. K. B. Green/Initial Photographics

Cardiff Railway 0-6-0ST 682 is at home at Cardiff East Dock shed in the early 1920s. The loco was rebuilt with Pannier Tanks in October 1926. The eight road shed forms a backdrop. Each road could accommodate eight tank locos. There was also a one road 'lifting shop'. To the left is Taff Vale O4 class 0-6-2T 285. Rail Archive Stephenson(Photomatic)

The same loco, Cardiff Railway 0-6-0PT 682 is at home on shed at Cardiff East Dock on 12 June 1948. Ray Hinton

Cardiff Railway 0-6-0PT 683 from Cardiff East Dock shed is at Caerphilly Works awaiting attention in the early 1950s. Anwell

Port Talbot Railway 0-6-0ST 812 is up on blocks with its wheels removed at Varteg Hill Colliery, near Pontypool in 1948. It was withdrawn in June 1934 and was purchased by Varteg Hill Colliery where it finally succumbed in 1950. Kenneth Brown

Two locos at home at Cardiff East Dock shed in the early 1950s are Rhymney Railway 0-6-0T 92 (previously 606) and 6705. Stanley J. Rhodes

Rhymney Railway 0-4-0Ts 120 and 121 were constructed as Railmotors. They were rebuilt as 0-6-0TTs in 1910 and were used as Pilot locos. GWR 661 is at home at Cardiff Docks in 1924 where it was shed Pilot. Withdrawal took place in February 1925.

Taff Vale Railway V class 0-6-0ST 789 is at Talywain shed in 1950. This loco was withdrawn in April 1930 and was sold via the Cymric Trading Co. to the Blaendare Co. Pontypool where it was named 'Blaendare'. In September 1948 it was transferred to Varteg Hill Colliery from where it moved to Talywain during 1949. Cutting up took place in September 1950. Kenneth Brown

Now we come to several photos of the three Taff Vale Railway 'Pwllyrhebog incline' H class 0-6-0Ts which were constructed with inclined Inner Firebox Crowns. To save repetition in the captions these became GWR 792 to 794 and were renumbered to 193 to 195. All were officially allocated to Treherbert shed. 792 is on the Turntable outside the original semi-roundhouse shed at Treherbert in the late 1920s. In February 1952 as 193 this loco was sold to the NCB Tar Distillation Works at Wernddu, Caerphilly where it was cut up in January 1960.

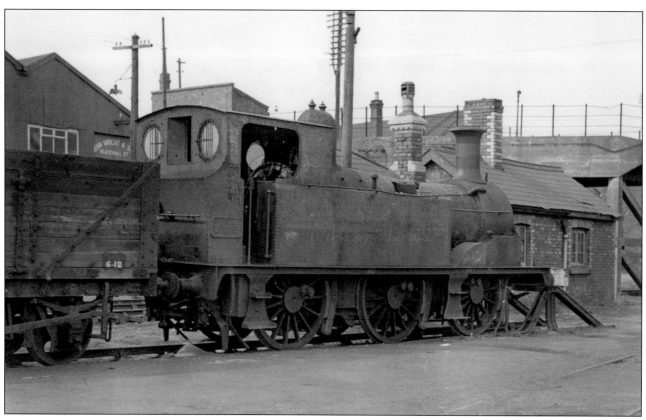

Having been around Cardiff East Dock shed on 21 April 1957 with time to spare I decided to wander around part of the docks area. I spied a loco in the distance and walked down to it. Imagine my delight when I was able to record 193 in use for Stationary Boiler duties at Roath West Basin. Use of this loco at this location has not been documented previously in any books. Maurice Dart/Transport Treasury

The same loco 193 is in company with 2021 class 0-6-0PT 2034 is at the Tar Works shed at Wernddu, Caerphilly in the late 1950s.

Taff Vale 194 shunts wagons at the foot of Pwllyrhebog Incline at Tonypandy in June1949. This loco was hired by Caerphilly Tar Works from November 1953 until May 1954. G. W. Sharpe & Co.

Taff Vale 194 keeps company with 0-6-2Ts at home at Treherbert shed on the coal stage road in the late 1940s.

Taff Vale 195 stands outside the small loco shed at the top of Pwllyrhebog Incline on 14 October 1949. In November 1951 this loco was sold to the NCB at Treorchy where it worked until scrapping took place in April 1957. On the left is GWR 20T Mineral wagon W109737. Potter

Taff Vale 195 gained a BR smokebox numberplate. It is working a train up Pwllyrhebog Incline in the early 1950s. These locos worked bunker first up the incline.

We end this section with LNER J66 class 0-6-0T 7292 shunting at Guest Keen & Baldwins East Moors yard at Cardiff Docks on 21 April 1957. The loco is carrying the GKB number 10. This was shortly after I had stumbled on Taff Vale 193 during my walk around the docks and I could not believe my luck. I crossed over some industrial lines and the loco started to reverse as I approached. The loco had been withdrawn by the LNER in October 1936 and worked here until January 1959. Coupled to the loco are Imperial Smelting Corporation Tank wagons 96, 194 and 83. Maurice Dart/Transport Treasury

18

FOUR COUPLED LOCOS

Details of the duties worked by each of these varied types are contained in the captions.

We commence this varied section with Taff Vale C class Passenger 4-4-2T 171 (GWR 1302) at Cathays shed in the early 1920s. This loco was withdrawn in August 1926. Just visible in the right background is part of Taff Vale M1 class 0-6-2T 71 (GWR 478) which worked until June 1925.

GWR Bulldog class 4-4-0s worked Passenger services on main line routes in the early part of the twentieth century and later found themselves employed on Parcels trains. In the 1920s Bulldog 3315 'QUANTOCK' waits on a through road at Cardiff General with a 4-6-0 for a path to Canton shed. The 4-4-0 which was allocated to Neyland shed in 1921 and was withdrawn in June 1931 had been rebuilt from Duke class 3324. The locos had detached from an Up working from west Wales.

Allocated to Stafford Road shed, Wolverhampton in 1921, Bulldog 3409 'QUEENSLAND' waits to depart from Cardiff General with an Up Passenger train in 1922. Withdrawal took place in January 1939. The Locomotive Club Of Great Britain/Ken Nunn Collection

Above left: Three Bulldogs lined up at Canton shed on 25 August 1935 are headed by un-named 3435 which was allocated to Neyland in 1934. This loco was a friend of mine as it was withdrawn from Laira in November 1945. In the left background is Dean Goods 0-6-0 2535 from St Phillips Marsh shed which worked until June 1946.

Above right: Allocated to Hereford shed in 1921 Bulldog 3447 'JACKDAW' waits to depart from Cardiff General in 1922 on an Up Passenger train. A working to Shrewsbury and the north of England the train is piloted by an unknown loco. The Locomotive Club Of Great Britain/Ken Nunn Collection

Passenger 3521 class 4-4-0 3538 waits to depart from Cardiff General with an Up working in the early 1920s. Allocated to Worcester this loco was withdrawn in July 1927. Railway Photographs

Rhymney Railway 62-66 class 2-4-2STs were Passenger locos for the first part of their life. Latterly GWR 1325 worked as Pilot loco at Caerphillly Works but was allocated to Cardiff Docks where it returned each evening. It is at Cardiff East Moors shed on 17 November 1923. Withdrawal took place in August 1928 and the loco was cut up in September 1929.

19

OIL-BURNERS AND SHED SCENES

During the coal shortage in the mid-1940s the GWR converted some locos of several types to burn oil fuel some of which were temporarily renumbered. Views of locos depots complete this section.

In 1947/48 2800 class 2-8-0 4806 (ex 2832) from Llanelly shed is on shed at Severn Tunnel Junction. This loco ran as an Oil-Burner from May 1946 until April 1949.

In the late 1940s 2800 class 2-8-0 4809 (ex 2845) from Old Oak Common shed rests between duties at Severn Tunnel Junction. This loco ran as an Oil-Burner from August 1947 until December 1949. Lens Of Sutton Collection

On 31 July 1946 2884 class 2-8-0 3818 (later 4852) from Severn Tunnel Junction shed enters Cardiff General with a Down Goods. As 4852 this loco was transferred to Laira in 1947 and ran as an Oil-Burner from January 1946 until September 1948. A. B. Harford

Lined up around the Turntable in Aberdare shed in 1959 are 5600 class 0-6-2T 6605, 4200 class 2-8-0T 4228, 4575 class 2-6-2T 4593, 5600 class 0-6-2T 6651, 8750 class 0-6-0PT 3655 and 5600 class 0-6-2T 5649. All were aloocated to Aberdare except 4593 which was a Pontypool Road engine. Rail Archive Stephenson(Photomatic)

This is an aerial view of remotely situated Dowlais Caeharris shed on 3 January 1959 with a 5600 class 0-6-2T outside. The newly built coaling plant is to the right of the shed. The running lines pass to the left of the shed and curve right into a cutting. Lines on the right serve the steel works. Stephenson Locomotive Society

My first visit to Caeharris shed was on 2 September 1957. I was most surprised to find this turntable at the rear of the shed. It was used to turn locos for snow plough work in the severe winters experienced in the area. The line to Cwmbargoed passed through the overline bridge in the centre of the photo.

In the mid-1950s Pannier tanks and 5600 class 0-6-2Ts occupy the coal stage road and yard at Cathays shed. The nearest loco is 7400 class 0-6-0PT 7445. Stephenson Locomotive Society

Many locos are lined up at Cathays shed on 21 April 1957. Identifiable on the left are resident 4575 class Auto-fitted 4580 and 4589 and local 7400 class 0-6-0PT 7445. Inside the shed on the right is BR 3MT 2-6-2T 82034 from Treherbert. Three 5600 class 0-6-2Ts are included. Maurice Dart

Three locos are inside the factory at Cathays shed on 6 May 1951. On the left is 5600 class 0-6-2T 5635 allocated to 88D which is probably Rhymney. Next are local residents 6400 class 0-6-0PT 6416 and Taff Vale A class 0-6-2T 371. H. C. Casserley

Two locos are outside coke ovens on 9 August 1931. On the right is 5600 class 0-6-2T 5643 which is at home. On the left is an unidentified Taff Vale 0-6-2T.

A. B. Crompton

This is Radyr shed on Bank Holiday Sunday afternoon 17 April 1960. All of the locos are at home unless a shed allocation is shown in brackets. On the left is 5101 class 2-6-2T 4160 which is preserved and operates on the West Somerset Railway. The long line of 5600 class 0-6-2Ts contains, 6608, 6648, 6626, 5618, 6682, and 5600 (Treherbert). In the third row are 9400 class 0-6-0PTs 3409, 8470 and 3402. On the right is visiting 4300 class 2-6-0 6377 from Carmarthen shed. Maurice Dart/Transport Treasury

Left: Visible at Rhymney shed around 11am on 28 August 1960 are local resident 5600 class 0-6-2Ts 5662, 5622, 5630, 5696, 5660 and 5681. Maurice Dart

20

BR DIESEL LOCOMOTIVES

A small selection of some of the types which worked in the area is included.

Having travelled from Plymouth to Newport by train I caught a bus to Pontllanffraith and set off to locate the Bird-in-Hand Inn after which a nearby complex junction had been named. After visiting the establishment I returned to Pontllanffraith and set off eastwards to attempt to obtain a photograph of Penar tunnel. A group of railwaymen were working on the track at Penar Junction and after a chat with them I walked to the tunnel and back to the junction where they told me that trains were due in each direction on the 'Hall's Road' route. I was permitted to find vantage points to record each train. In the afternoon on 9 November 1967 1750hp class 37 Co-Co Diesel Electric D6904 (later 37204 and 37378) from Canton depot brings empty coal wagons off the Lower section of Hall's Road at Penar Junction bound for Markham Colliery. Maurice Dart

Right: On 1 July 1978 Canton depot's 37280 (ex D6980) stands in the yard at Aberdare High Level. Maurice Dart

In the afternoon on 9 November 1967 the first train at Penar Junction came down the Upper section of Hall's Road from Markham Colliery hauled by Canton depot's D6990 (later 37290 and 37411). Maurice Dart

On 28 July 1976 a triple headed empty iron ore train from Llanwern Steelworks to Port Talbot heads west through Newport station. It is hauled by 37307 (ex D6607, later 37403), 37306 (ex D6606, later 37273, 37306, 37273) and 37303 (ex D6603, later 37271, 37333). All of the locos were based at Landore depot.

3250hp Co-Co Diesel Electric class 56 56083 from Canton depot brings a long Freight east through Newport on 21 November 2003. Maurice Dart

3100hp Co-Co Diesel Electric class 60 60077 from Canton depot heads west through Newport on a Freight on 21 November 2003. Maurice Dart

Canton allocated 350hp Diesel Electric shunter 08191 (ex D3260) rests in the yard at Aberdare High Level on 1 July 1978. Maurice Dart

On 21 November 2003 09102 (ex D4000, 08832) from Canton depot brings a wagon through Newport transferring it from East Usk yard to Alexandra Dock Junction yard. Maurice Dart

21

TRACK SCENES, TUNNELS AND VIADUCTS

This section consists of a few unusual track scenes followed by shots of the more impressive tunnels and viaducts in the area.

Above left: We commence with the Great Western bridge which was south of the GWR station at Ebbw Vale Low Level and carried a Steel Works line over the GWR lines. This view dates from the early 1920s. A. Bowen

Above right: This is a view looking off the north side of Walnut Tree viaduct which I took from the Noon Rhymney to Barry Island excursion train on 28 August 1960. Just beyond the overline bridge is Taffs Well station. Diverging to the right is the line which climbed to Penrhos Junction on which a 5600 class 0-6-2T is standing in a loop with a short PW train. Beyond the station the line diverging to the right is the branch line to Nantgarw. On the far right is the trackbed of the Cardiff Railway route to Nantgarw and Treforest. Maurice Dart/Transport Treasury

Left: I took this shot from the 5pm Pontypool Road to Neath train after it had departed from Pontllanffraith Low Level on 18 August 1962. It shows part of the complex layout at Bird-in-Hand Junction. Uppermost, curving left is the Sirhowy Valley line from Pontllanffraith High Level to Risca. Centre is Tredegar Junction Lower where the line from Sirhowy Junction curved in to join it. That cut off line closed in 1967. The Sirhowy Valley line closed in 1970. The line I was riding closed in 1964. Maurice Dart/Transport Treasury

This is the south portal of 1868yd Wenvoe tunnel which I took from a Pontypridd to Barry Island train on 26 June 1960. This route closed in 1962. Maurice Dart/Transport Treasury

Below: In the late 1900s 4-6-0 4002 'EVENING STAR' brings a Down train out from the Welsh portal of 7668yd Severn Tunnel. Locomotive Publishing Co. Ltd.

This is the south portal of the abandoned Cardiff Railway 180yd Tongwynlais (Castle Coch) tunnel in 1963. The route through this tunnel closed in 1931. This tunnel has been lost due to modern road construction.

Here is an early photograph of the west portal of the abandoned Taff Vale Extension 703yd Quaker's Yard (Cefn Glas) tunnel which closed in 1964.

On 9 November 1967 I walked from Pontllanffraith to Penar Junction and a short way down Hall's Road Lower Section to photograph the north portal of 239yd Penar Tunnel, traffic through which ceased in 1989. Maurice Dart

On 5 June 1971 the Inspector at Barry island gave me permission to walk down the track to photograph the east portal of the Barry Railway's 280yd Barry Island tunnel traffic through which ceased in 1975. He told me that I was welcome to walk through it but unfortunately time prevented me from doing so. Maurice Dart

The magnificent Crumlin Viaduct on the Taff Vale Extension route around 1900. 553yd long and 200ft high the line over it closed on 15 June 1964. The Wrench Series

Another masterpiece of construction was the Barry Railway's Llanbradach viaduct on the line to New Tredegar. 125ft high with a length of 800yd closure took place on 4 August 1926. The structure was demolished in 1937 but one pier remained at the west end in 1960.

Another impressive Barry Railway viaduct was Walnut Tree which spanned the Taff Valley between Penrhos Junction and Walnut Tree Tunnel. I took this shot from the 'Rambling 56' Railtour on 31 July 1965. Traffic across this 516yd long 120ft high structure ceased on 14 December 1967. The girders were removed in 1969 and the piers were demolished in 1973.
Maurice Dart

This is the remains of the Barry Railway Penyrheol viaduct taken from a train on the Senghenydd branch on 27 August 1960. 50ft high with a length of 185yd closure took place in 1926 with partial demolition occurring in 1937. Maurice Dart

This is the Rhymney Railway's 111yd long Bargoed Viaduct on 31 July 1965. Maurice Dart

Below: This section ends with a somewhat complex railway scene. On the left with track 'in situ' is 173yd Hall's Viaduct which was on Hall's Road Lower Section north of Cross Keys which closed in 1989. To its right on the original alignment is the long disused Hall's Tramroad's Pantywaun Viaduct. In the foreground is the branch line to Cwmcarn Colliery which closed in 1968. Hidden from view in the valley passing below each viaduct is the Western Valleys line to Crumlin Low Level. J.A. Peden

22
INDUSTRIAL LOCOMOTIVES

A selection of these types which worked in the area is included here.

Ex Wantage Tramway 0-4-0ST No.7 (MW 1057/1888) is at the Dos Works, Cordes Steel Mills, Newport on 27 July 1960. This veteran was scrapped in December 1963.

After visiting Tredegar shed on 2 September 1957 I walked around the NCB lines north of the station. Moving around was 0-4-0ST No.5 (HL 2463/1900). Tredegar station is in the left background. Maurice Dart/Transport Treasury

This loco working at Allied Steel & Wire (ex GKN), Cardiff Docks in July 1949 carried no identification except its builders plate. Using an ultra-strong magnifier coupled with it carrying no other number I have identified this loco as 0-6-0ST (P 653/1896). It was allocated No.5 but this was never applied. It was scrapped in 1961. L. R. Peters

Guest Keen & Baldwins 0-6-0ST No.24 (HE 3718/ 1950) moves wagons around the Steel Works at East Moors, Cardiff Docks on 21 April 1957. Maurice Dart/Transport Treasury

Whilst on a train from Cardiff Queen Street to Caerphilly on 27 August 1960 I saw a loco at the Tar Works at Wernddu. Having spent the night at Caerphilly, before setting off to Rhymney I walked to the Tar Works. There, after some protracted questioning I was taken to see the loco. Apparently the works had suffered a fire a few days earlier resulting in visitors being discouraged. On 28 August 1960 0-4-0ST 'LUCIFER' (HL 3168/1916) is at the Tar Works. Maurice Dart/Transport Treasury

I was aware that there was a second loco at the Tar Works and after some minutes persuading my guide of the importance of photographing it I was taken on quite a long walk to see it. Resting inside the small loco shed at the Tar Works on 28 August 1960 is 0-4-0ST 'ROSE No.1' (AE 1863/1921). Maurice Dart/Transport Treasury

I saw this diminutive loco from a train from Caerphilly to Rhymney on 28 August 1960. As I returned on the Noon excursion from Rhymney to Barry Island I photographed it from the train. The loco, 4wD MR 1946/1919 is at Welsh Metal Industries Ltd south west of Aber Junction. My train which was not booked to call at Caerphilly, was traversing the non-passenger line from Aber Junction to Penrhos Junction. The works are adjacent to the site of the first Caerphilly station. Maurice Dart/Transport Treasury

As I was riding a train from Caerphilly to Senghenydd on 27 June 1960 I passed the remains of a scrapped loco in a derelict shed at Windsor Colliery, Abertridwr. As I returned along the branch I took this shot from the train of 0-4-0ST 'KITCHENER' (AB 1372/1914). The boiler which was upside down with the firebox uppermost presented this sad sight. Maurice Dart/Transport Treasury

On 4 April 1969 0-6-0ST 'GLENDOWER' (HE 3810/1954) shunts wagons at Hafodyrynys Colliery. This loco has been preserved at the South Devon Railway at Buckfastleigh. The running line to Pontypool Road virtually ran through the centre of this colliery. Maurice Dart/Transport Treasury

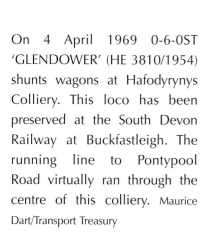

I took this shot from the 5pm Pontypool Road to Neath train on 18 August 1962 as it passed the loco shed at Ocean & Taff Merthyr Colliery. Standing outside the shed is 0-4-0ST 'TAFF MERTHYR No.3' (AB 2371/1955). Maurice Dart

On 17 April 1978 a rake of empty coal wagons from Penrikyber approaches Mountain Ash hauled by 0-6-0ST No.8 (RSH 7139/1944 Rblt HE 3880/1961). This loco has been preserved at the Pontypool & Blaenavon Railway. This section of line which was once part of the High Level route from Penrhiwceiber to Aberdare was taken over by the NCB following closure by BR. Maurice Dart/Transport Treasury

Whilst I was visiting Caeharris shed on 2 September 1957 I heard a steam loco working hard so I exited the shed and I. C. I. Dowlais's 0-4-0ST 'JENNIFER' (WB 1667/1942) came storming up the steeply graded line from a section of the Works lower down the hill. Maurice Dart/Transport Treasury

As I left Dowlais Caeharris station to walk to Dowlais Central on 2 September 1957 a train was approaching Caeharris from the Guest Keen & Nettelfolds Works hauled by almost new 0-4-0D No.2 (HC D1030/1957). Maurice Dart/Transport Treasury

On 26 June 1960 I took this shot from a passing train of NCB 0-4-0ST (P1171/1910) at Firw Branch Colliery, Trehafod.
Maurice Dart/Transport Treasury

Below: Also on 26 June 1960, from the same train I photographed 0-6-0ST 'TYNYCOED' (P 1679/1929) at the NCB Fodder Store at Llwynypia. *Maurice Dart/Transport Treasury*

In this marvellous photo an unidentified 0-4-0ST hauls a works train, apparently locally called 'The Mail' carrying staff during the construction of Grwyne Fawr Reservoir north west of Llanvihangel in the 1920s. Maurice Dart Collection/Transport Treasury

LOCATION INDEX